Every Time I Blow My Top I Lose My Head!

A KID'S GUIDE TO KEEPING COOL UNDER STRESS

Formerly *Take a Deep Breath: The Kid's Play-Away Stress Book*

CALL 1·800·962·1141

A Brand of The Guidance Group
www.guidance-group.com

Every Time I Blow My Top I Lose My Head!

By Laura Slap-Shelton, Psy.D. and Lawrence E. Shapiro, Ph.D.
Illustrated by Bob Beckett

Childswork/Childsplay is a catalog of products for mental health professionals, techers, and parents who wish to help children with their social and emotional growth.

Childswork/Childsplay grants limited permnission for the copying of this publication to its customers for their individual professional use. Permission for publication for any other use must be obtained in writing from the publisher.

© 1992. 1999 Childswork/Childsplay
A Brand of The Guidance Group
www.guidance-group.com

All rights reserved.
Printed in the United States of America

ISBN 10: 1-882732-82-0
ISBN 13: 978-1-882732-82-1

HOW TO USE THIS BOOK

Every Time I Blow My Top I Lose My Head is an instructional book designed to teach children about dealing with stress. It can be read straight through, but most likely children will want to do each activity that they read about, so it might take several sittings to finish. Some children may get distracted from the "lessons" of the book and wish to talk about other things or try out some of the ideas. To some extent, this should be allowed.

Play is the most natural stress reducer for children (as well as adults), and we believe that learning to handle upset feelings and stressful situations should not in itself be stressful. If the child resists the structured activities included in the book, you should read the book aloud and perform the activities yourself. Children are quick to imitate adults and will soon join in the fun.

Every Time I Blow My Top I Lose My Head covers the most common techniques used with children to help them cope with stress, but this book can only introduce these techniques. The methods described in the book will be most effective if they are used *at the time and in the place* where the problem is occurring and if they are encouraged by a supportive and caring adult.

We urge you to read the section FOR PARENTS AND OTHER CAREGIVERS and to explore ways that you can reduce stress in your own life. If you know a child who is under a great deal of stress, we also urge you to read the section WHEN TO SEEK PROFESSIONAL HELP FOR CHILDREN UNDER STRESS. Every child has a different capacity in learning to cope with stress, and some may need professional guidance.

We hope that you and the children you care about enjoy this book and benefit from its lessons. So find a comfortable chair, take a deep breath, and READ!

WHAT IS STRESS?

Some days, everything seems to go your way. Everything happens just as you wish. You get an "A" on a test. You're popular. You have fun with your brother or sister. You're elected captain of the team. Your parents tell you how proud they are of you.

On these days, you can handle just about anything.

But then, there are those other days, when life seems pretty tough. Nothing seems to go your way. You get a low grade on a test. Your best friend ignores you on the bus. You don't get to play on the team you want to be on. You fight with your brother or sister. And your parents get angry with you.

On those days, you may feel angry, sad, grouchy—or all three!

On those days, *just one more thing* might be too much to handle.

On those hard days, you are feeling STRESS!

Stress is invisible. Nobody can see it. But when it gets really bad, you can definitely see its effects.

Some people say that stress makes them feel like they are being S T R E T C H E D too far.

Imagine you had clay and you rolled it into a fat snake. Then you took each end of the snake and pulled until the snake became thinner and thinner. Eventually, it would break. That's how it feels sometimes when you are stressed.

Some people say that stress feels like they are being hit over the head with a hammer. Others say that angry feelings make them feel like they are going to explode into a hundred pieces.

Some people think that if they can be strong enough or tough enough or cool enough, then stress won't bother them. But they are wrong. *Everyone* feels stress, and everyone gets angry at times—tall people, short people, rich people, poor people, kids, parents, teachers, doctors, cowboys—everyone.

Stress isn't good or bad. It is just a part of life. Having stress doesn't mean that you are not happy. Look at your parents, for example. Having children can be very stressful. Parents have to work to make money so they can get you the things you need and want. They worry if you are sick or if you have problems. They try very hard to do the right things to make you happy and smart.

Being a parent can be very stressful, but most parents are very happy to be parents, and they don't mind the stress—at least not most of the time, they don't.

Anger and stress can come from two directions: from *outside* you and from *inside* you.

Here are some of the things from the outside that can cause you to feel stressed:
- getting your fingers caught in a door
- losing a race
- being teased
- getting a bad grade
- practicing the piano
- getting a shot from the doctor.

Can you think of three things from the outside that made you feel stressed this week?

Try to picture in your mind someone (or something) from the outside that causes you stress. For example:

- your big sister
- homework
- a bully
- someone in the house who yells a lot

Draw that person or thing in the space below. Don't worry about how good your drawing is. Just get something down on paper. Color it in, if you like.

Stress can also come from the inside—from your feelings. Here are some feelings that can make you feel stressed:
- being angry at your best friend
- being ashamed about something you said
- feeling sad because someone you care about is not around
- being jealous of the way another kid looks
- being afraid of the big dog in your neighbor's yard.

Can you think of a time when you were really stressed because of the way you felt?

Feelings come from the inside, but they show on the outside. When someone is sad, happy, mad, or afraid, you usually know it.

Can you draw some faces that show these emotions? Again, don't worry about how good your drawing is. Have fun with it.

HOW DO WE RECOGNIZE STRESS?

Often, we don't even know when we are feeling stress. Sometimes we get so used to feeling stress that we think that feeling bad is just normal. But once you know about stress, there are lots of ways to tell if you, or someone you know, is "stressed out."

There are three important things that can tell you that you have stress:

    1. Your feelings.
    2. The way your body looks and feels.
    3. Your behavior.

Everyone has many different feelings. Some feelings make us feel good, and some feelings make us feel bad.

The feelings that make us feel bad can be caused by stress. When people feel stress, they can be *afraid*, *irritable*, *angry*, *tired*, *sad*, or many other things. For example, if you keep striking out at baseball every time you go to bat, you may feel *embarrassed* that people saw you fail, or you may feel *guilty* because you let your team down.

Not being good enough at something is a stress that we all know. After all, nobody's perfect. Our bad feelings tell us that we are under stress.

If you can put a name to your feelings, then you can probably figure out why you feel that way, and you can change those feelings. Changing negative feelings to positive feelings is one way to deal with stress.

These are some of the feelings and examples of those feelings that can tell you that you are stressed:

Guilty: Mike knows he should not have stolen that candy bar.

Pressured: Amanda never has any time to do her homework.

Hurried: Bob is always late for the school bus.

Shame: Ralph is ashamed of the way he talked back to his mother.

Feeling Unimportant: Sam feels that he isn't as good as his big brother.

Frustrated: Dan doesn't play basketball very well, but he loves to play anyway.

Overwhelmed: Sally doesn't understand her math homework.

Bored: Barbara hates practicing the piano.

Can you think of some things that these kids could do to change their negative feelings into positive ones? You can write them down if you want to.

1. _____

2. _____

3. _____

Do you have any feelings right now that are telling you that you are stressed? What are they? What can you do about them?

1. _____

2. _____

3. _____

Playing is an important way for kids (and grown-ups) to deal with stress. Play helps us express ourselves, relieve tension, take our mind off things…and it's fun!

Sometimes you can look at someone who is playing and see that they are working off stress. People who play sports can often work off their stress on the field. Board games, card games, or hobbies can relieve stress by focusing our minds on something more calming.

Play can also help us deal with stress because it encourages us to be creative and imaginative.

Build something. You can use blocks or clay or books or dominoes. Make a scary monster out of felt or a paper bag. Creating something out of raw materials can be a great way to relieve stress. Below, draw a picture of what you would like to build.

Stress can be moderate or intense. When you are under a moderate amount of stress, you may start to notice different things about yourself. You may seem more tired than usual, or you may have trouble falling asleep. You may feel cranky or irritable. You may not have much energy, or you may be very, very active.

When you are under a lot of stress, your body lets you know. It can:

- hurt and give you headaches or stomach aches;
- make your heart beat very, very fast, so that it feels like it is pounding in your chest;
- make you breathe very fast, so that you feel like you can't catch your breath.

Below, draw a picture of yourself under stress.

When they were asked what made them feel like they were under a lot of stress, this is what some kids said:

"When I had to go to the hospital and have an operation."

"When my uncle died and I went to his funeral."

"When my teacher made me stand up in front of the whole class and tell them that I had taken Marty's money."

Can you think of some times when you were under a lot of stress?

Our behavior (the things we do) can tell us that we are under stress. For example, sometimes when kids are under stress they do things they might not normally do.

Sometimes they watch more TV.

Sometimes they don't play with their friends.

Sometimes they can't concentrate on their homework.

Most of the time it's hard for kids to see that they are acting differently because of stress. But other people may notice the difference.

Here are some things that grownups have noticed about kids who were under stress:

"Danny was very quiet in class all of a sudden."

"Chantal didn't pay any attention when her mom talked to her."

"José didn't want to see any of his friends."

"Karen didn't seem to want to talk to her parents about anything."

LEARNING TO DEAL WITH STRESS

Now you know that stress is a part of life that affects everyone. You know the signs of stress and that these signs can be warning signals, just the way signs on the road can be warning signals.

Now it is time to learn *how* to deal with stress; to learn how to *cope* with it. When you learn to cope with something, you learn to adjust to it in a positive way.

For example, when it is very hot outside, you wear cool clothing and you stay out of the sun. When you can, you take a swim or run under the sprinkler. That's coping with the heat. You can't make the heat go away (although it will eventually), so you learn to adjust to it.

Probably the best way to cope with stress is to learn to relax. *Really* relax.

Relaxing when you are feeling stress is like going into an air-conditioned room when it is hot outside. It helps you cope *right away*, and it makes your "stress meter" go down for a long time afterwards. (My stress meter, as you can see, is going down as I write this.)

But relaxing when you are under stress is not as easy as it sounds. It takes some practice.

Begin by sitting down in a comfortable chair or on a soft carpet surrounded by pillows.

The next thing to do may seem funny, because it is the opposite of being relaxed. Try your hardest to be tense, to tighten your muscles as hard as you can.

Clench your fists very tightly.
Now let go, and open your hands.

Notice how your hands feel now.
They are more relaxed than when you began.

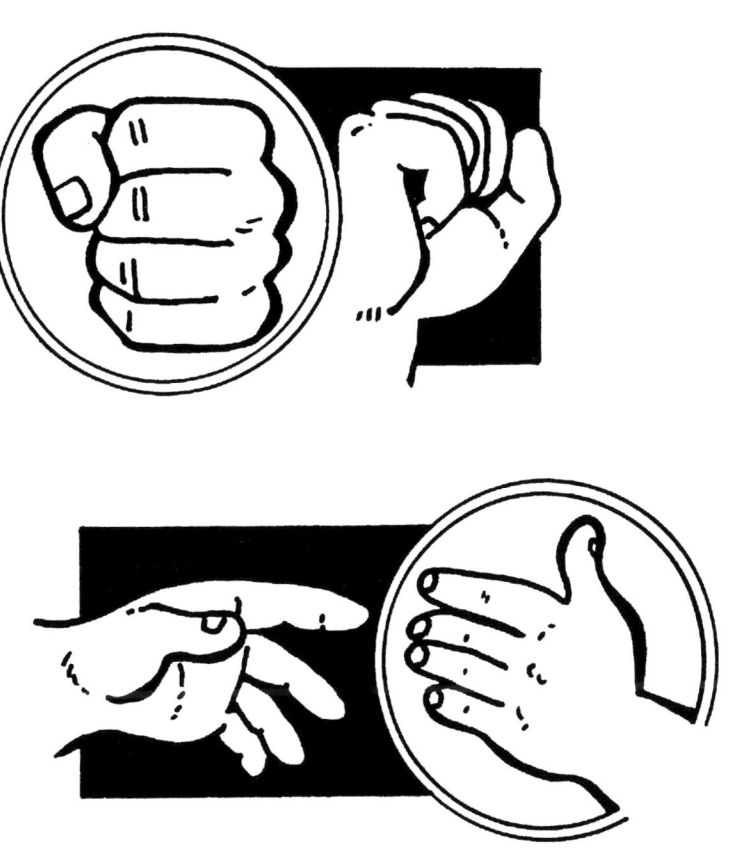

Practice tensing and relaxing using a squishy ball. Squeeze it as tightly as you can in your fist. Now relax your hand completely, so that the ball just flops right out of it.

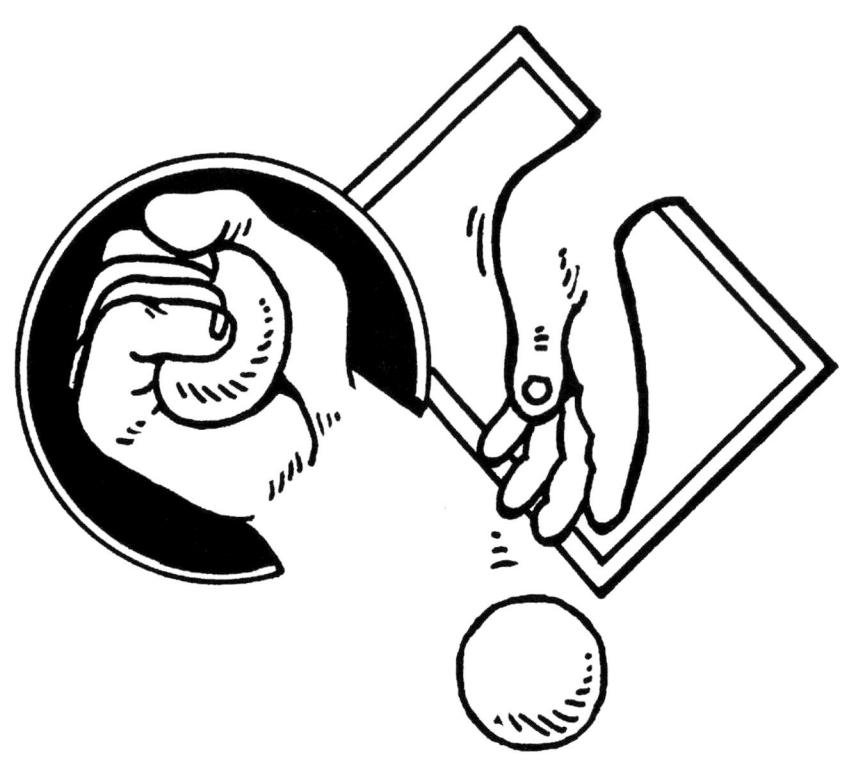

To learn to completely relax, you must practice tensing and relaxing one part of your body at a time. When you tense, count to 10 slowly. When you relax, count to 20 slowly.

• • • • • • • • • • •

FOR YOUR HEAD
Make the scariest face you can.
Now let it go and relax your face.

FOR YOUR ARMS
Stretch them out like you are going to fly. Hold your arms steady and tighten all your muscles. Now bring your arms down to your sides and let them rest there, like they are bags of heavy sand.

FOR YOUR BODY
Squeeze everything at once, like you are a ball of clay and someone is squeezing you! Now let all your muscles go at once and go limp, like you are a big, floppy rag doll.

FOR YOUR LEGS AND FEET
Hold your legs up off the ground as long as you can. Scrunch your toes at the same time. Now let go and let your feet flop down, like they are heavy weights.

• • • • • • • • • • •

Some kids have difficulty learning to tense and relax their bodies. If you can, get someone to help you tense and relax one part of your body at a time.

Here is another thing that you can do to help you relax. It is very easy because you do it all the time…breathe!

When you are tense, you automatically take shorter breaths. Just like when you are running very hard, when your body is tense it tries to get a lot of fresh oxygen by breathing quickly.

Taking a super-deep breath or two is the fastest way to slow down and relax. When you breathe *deeply* and *slowly*, it also helps you relax your muscles.

Let's do it now...

Breathe in as much air as you can. Imagine that your lungs are balloons, and fill them up. Hold the air for about six seconds (counting very slowly).

And then let it out.

Very slowly, let the balloon deflate, until all the air is out.

Now breathe normally again. Can you tell the difference?

Now try it again. Take a very deep breath, fill your chest up with air, like a balloon. Now hold the air in for six seconds…

Let it out slowly. Let your body relax.

Can you feel the stress floating away?

There's one more trick to learning to relax and get rid of stress.

Just like relaxing your body, and like breathing, you already know how to do this. It's called IMAGINATION!

Imagination is like making a picture in your mind. You probably do this all the time.

When you imagine a picture of yourself relaxing in your mind, your level of stress actually goes down. The more you concentrate on seeing yourself relaxed, the more you actually feel relaxed.

Close your eyes and try to imagine yourself relaxing…on the beach, floating in a pool—whatever feels good to you.

See yourself on the beach again.
Can you feel the warm sand?
Can you smell the salt air?
Can you hear the sea gulls?

Really concentrate. Does it almost seem like you are there? Take a very deep breath now and, as you let it out, feel very relaxed.

You can imagine yourself anywhere you like that is calm and peaceful. How about lying in a big park, looking up at the clouds?

What does it feel like? What do you hear? What do you smell?

Many people use imagination to help them relax. These are some of the things that people imagine:

- floating on a cloud;
- sitting in a room full of warm, golden light;
- floating away in a big balloon.

There is one more thing that you can do to help yourself relax anytime you like. Talk to yourself!

Say things that make you feel good, peaceful, and calm. Tell yourself:

"I feel very calm."

"I love myself."

"My mind is peaceful and clear."

"I am a special person."

"My parents and friends love me."

"I can solve my own problems."

All four of these things can help you relax and cope with stress. But the best way to relax and deal with stress is to use them all together!

Try this: Find a comfortable chair that reclines or put some pillows on the floor to lie down on.

Relax all the muscles in your body. First tighten and relax the muscles in your face, your arms, your body, your legs.

Now relax all the muscles in your body so that it feels heavy but good.

Take a very deep breath, hold it in, and let it out very slowly.

Now do it again and, as you let the air out, feel yourself becoming more and more relaxed.

Close your mind and think of yourself in a very relaxing place. Concentrate on it very hard. See if you can hear, smell, and feel what that place is like.

Now that you are very relaxed, say some things that will make you feel good about yourself.

Some kids are under more stress than others.

Listed below are a few situations that cause stress for kids:

- Kids whose parents are getting divorced are under a lot of stress.

- Kids who have an illness or who are dealing with a death in the family are under a lot of stress.

- Kids who have trouble in school are under a lot of stress.

If you are under a lot of stress, then you should practice these relaxation exercises every day.

Learning to relax is like learning almost anything. The more you practice, the better you will be at it.

If you practice these relaxation exercises you can learn to relax very quickly, even if you are under a lot of stress…even if you are waiting to get a shot from the doctor…even if you are about to take a test…even if you are about to sing a song in front of the whole school. And so on.

Just say to yourself, *I can relax*. Take a deep breath, and feel relaxed just the way you practiced.

LIVING A LOW-STRESS LIFE

Relaxing is an important way to deal with the stress that you are feeling right now. But there are things you can do every day to keep your stress level at a low level all the time.

First, you have to take good care of yourself.

You wouldn't want to be like Tim. Tim wakes up late for school every day. Some days he has a donut for breakfast, and some days he doesn't eat anything. Usually he hasn't finished his homework, so he has to do it on the school bus.

He watches TV all the time and stays up as late as he can.

He hates fruits and vegetables and eats candy and snack food between meals.

He likes to play video games, and he doesn't go outside or exercise unless someone makes him do it.

Tim is leading a high-stress life.

Eating a lot of sugary food and snack foods makes your body feel stressed.

Watching TV and playing video games for hours every day makes your mind feel stressed.

Staying up late and rushing around all the time causes a lot of stress.

It's better to be more like Cathy, who sets her alarm the night before, dresses herself quickly in the morning, eats a healthy breakfast, and still has enough time to be at the bus stop to talk to her friends.

After school, she gets her homework done, plays with her friends or goes to an after-school activity, eats dinner with her family, and watches a little TV before bed. When she's tired, she goes to sleep, even if it's *before* her bedtime.

Cathy is leading a low-stress life, and she feels great!

You can lead a low-stress life if you remember:

Good nutrition helps the body work well.
Getting enough rest helps the body work well.
Getting exercise helps the body work well.
Being organized and responsible helps you not to be rushed.

This book has helped you learn a bit about stress—what it is, how to recognize it, how to deal with it, and how to live a low-stress lifestyle. You've learned that being stressed-out isn't fun at all, and being relaxed and happy with your life feels a lot better.

You've got the ability to choose what's best for you.
So take a deep breath, stay cool under pressure, and choose wisely.

FOR PARENTS AND OTHER CAREGIVERS

This book is designed to be shared with your child. The ideas and exercises in it require some discussion and practice. But this book, in and of itself, cannot really reduce stress in the child's life. That is up to you.

THE WORLD IS A STRESSFUL PLACE

These days it is very difficult to provide our children with the stress-free life that was the ideal of child-rearing just a few decades ago. The modern world is full of many alarming and distressing problems, including AIDS, homelessness, drugs, child abductions, and violence at all levels of society. As much as we would like to protect our children from these concerns, it is unrealistic to think we can do this.

Our children learn about the world in school, on the playground, and, of course, from watching TV and seeing movies. Changes in the family, even subtle ones, are probably the most common causes of stress. Attempting to pretend that everything is all right actually creates more stress in children, as they come to feel unprotected by their "blissfully ignorant" parents.

Children are often the recipients of the stress that parents bring home. As a parent, you are stressed by the demands of balancing work, child rearing, and marriage. If you are a single parent, there are additional stressors. When parents are stressed, their children feel it.

You may not have the time or patience your children need. You may hurry your children along to keep up with the carefully arranged schedule of the day without regard to their internal schedule. You may tend to raise your voice more often and find yourself arguing more with your children than you'd like. You may not be able to fully listen to your children's concerns because you're overwhelmed with your own worries. You may realize that these things create stress for your children, but, like most of us, you find it difficult to change them.

Children also have stress that is related to their own development and the age-appropriate challenges they face every day. These stressors change with each passage to a new stage of maturity, and the change in itself is stressful. Children must face the normal pressures of becoming more independent from their parents, performing in school, gaining acceptance by teachers and peers, and so on.

The Hurried Child by David Elkind (Addison Wesley, 1988) is an eye-opening book for many parents who don't realize how even their best intentions for their children can create more stress. When children run from school to soccer practice to piano practice to ballet practice they can experience the same stress as overworked adults.

Elkin describes the most stressed child as the one who is forced to behave like an adult well before he or she has had a chance to develop the necessary maturity—before he or she has had a childhood. We see this trend played out in TV commercials that depict children playing the roles of overextended, hurried "parents," encouraging their "children" to eat a good breakfast, eat their vegetables, wear appropriate clothes for work, etc.

All this stress takes a tangible toll on our children; hence, an increasing number of children suffer from chronic stress-related illnesses. The rate of heart disease in American children is the highest in the world. Next to heart disease, asthma, which most doctors agree has stress-related factors, is the most prevalent form of childhood illness.

Psychologists and behavioral symptoms of stress in children include, but are not limited to, anorexia nervosa and obesity, drug and alcohol abuse, fatigue, low frustration tolerance, depression, low self-esteem, delinquency, aggression, poor school attendance, academic underachievement, and poor concentration.

A PROGRAM FOR SUCCESS

All this may seem like depressing news. But the good news is that there are ways you can reduce stress in the lives of your children and things you can teach them that will help them deal with a lifetime of stress.

Begin by acknowledging what causes you to be stressed. The causes of your stress will most likely have a direct or indirect effect on your children.

Next, identify those things that cause stress for each individual child. When you are aware of an upcoming event that you think is likely to be stressful for your child, the best thing you can do is discuss it with your child before it happens. Preparing children for a stressful event gives them time to start building some coping strategies and removes the extra stress that comes with surprises.

Prepare for major stressful events as early as possible. These would include the birth of a sibling; beginning school for the first time; beginning a new grade; beginning at a new school; any sort of major medical procedure; moving to a new neighborhood; the expected death of a pet or relative; and separation or divorce of the parents.

As you discuss the event you will want to be careful to find out the child's view of it. Depending on the age of your child, you may be surprised at his or her idiosyncratic understanding of it. You can clarify your child's misconceptions by clearing up misunderstandings and providing basic facts. In order to help your child place the event in context, you will want to discuss the meaning of the event relative to the child as well as to other people affected by this particular stress.

For example, in preparation for the birth of a new baby, parents should look for opportunities to assure their older children that they will be loved no less once their sibling arrives. In the case of school preparation, it often helps to take your child to the school before it opens, to help him or her feel familiar. Some schools have initiated home visits from the teacher before school begins. Find out if this is a possibility for you.

In the case of illness or frightening medical procedures, it is important to let your child know what is going to happen and why it is going to happen. Plan to be with your child as much as possible while he or she is in the hospital. Have the doctor explain the procedure to your child.

For all upcoming events your child will benefit from having opportunities to express his or her feelings and ideas. Young children can benefit by having opportunities to "play act" the event. Slightly older children can benefit from hearing or reading stories related to the upcoming event. In these stories, a child typically experiences a similar stressful event (first day at school, a divorce, a death in the family, and so on) and successfully copes with it.

Sometimes a few effective changes in the child's environment can reduce the level of stress. The overall goal of these changes is to provide a more supportive structure for your child. Occasionally, simply helping your child to keep his or her room more orderly, and keeping the house more orderly, can bring some relief. Creating a more organized delegation of household chores, and a more organized schedule, may help. A more organized household will save you time and stress as well.

Parents must also pay attention to the stress that television brings into the house. Violent or "mature" TV shows can in themselves be stressful to a child, but even just sitting in front of a TV, hour after hour, can be a passive stressor. Time spent in front of a TV is time away from physical activities that promote strong bodies, playtime with friends that encourage the development of social skills, and time alone with parents, from which children can derive comfort and support.

Try to limit the number of hours your children spend watching TV. Encourage alternative activities, such as playing games, reading, or a hobby. Help your children to select nonviolent, child-oriented programs. Watch some of the shows with them in order to add a more mature perspective to their understanding of what they see. By establishing control over the television, you provide a more secure environment for your children. Taking the time to monitor what they watch will enable you to use television as a tool to promote their growth and well-being, rather than as a babysitter and social substitute.

Diet is also an important part of a child's inner environment. Government dietary recommendations encourage diets low in fat and high in complex carbohydrates. Children have more energy and are less prone to stress-induced illness when their diets are healthy and balanced. Use whole grain breads and cereals, minimize sugar, and offer fruits, nuts, or low-fat cheese for snacks when possible.

Set a good example for your children. This is not to say that you need to be excessively rigid. You will help them to improve their diets simply by not having high-sugar and high-fat foods in your house. For children with significant weight problems, it is best to consult a specialist and work out a diet to which your child will agree. In all cases, educate your children about the importance of the foods they eat.

Along with diet comes exercise. Many American children do not get enough exercise. Exercise reduces fatigue, increases self-confidence, and sharpens thinking, in addition to building strong bodies. Because of all these benefits, it is a terrific stress reducer! If you exercise or are involved with activities at a health club, why not include your children? Encourage their involvement in extracurricular sports and activities. Along with the more traditional sports, there is walking, biking, swimming, dancing, gymnastics, karate, skating, and bowling, among others, to choose from.

SCHOOL AS SOURCE OF STRESS

As we can all recall, school is often a big source of stress. School is the center of your child's life outside the family, and sometimes it will seem like the single most important thing in your child's life. By becoming an active listener you can find out about your child's experiences in school. Make a point of asking how things went each day and really listening to your child's answers.

If your child has concerns, become a partner in helping to figure out solutions. These solutions will not always involve you directly. At times, you may need only to encourage better use of peer support, or to suggest a graceful way out of a sticky situation. At other times, you may need to contact the teacher or school principal. Know what your child's homework assignments are, and make sure that time after school is allocated for homework.

If you feel that your child is having serious problems and you are not sure of the best way to help, then get help for yourself. Talk to your friends, your child's teacher or school counselor, or a professional counselor outside of the school. Finally, if you have time, you may want to participate in the PTA or other groups involved with improving your child's educational experience.

COMMUNICATING TO REDUCE STRESS

Communication can both create and relieve stress. As parents, a major part of our communication with our children involves issues around discipline. Disciplining children is an art. Positive discipline without use of physical punishment is the most productive way in which to help your child learn self-control and form the basis of self-esteem that well disciplined behavior implies. Try having your child take a "time-out" if you find that his or her behavior requires some correction. Calmly explain why he or she is receiving the time-out and let the child know how long it will be. During this time do something to help you relax, too!

Find opportunities to praise good behavior, rather than exert control by punishing bad behavior. Always let your children know that there is a difference between them and their behavior. Let them know that while you may be angry at something they did, you still love them. Knowing what is age-appropriate for your child, and in particular what is the best that your child can do, will free you to share in accomplishments without weighing their value on inaccurate scales.

Friends can provide a lot of good ideas and support for your disciplining efforts. They will recognize your desire to be a good parent and will encourage you and amuse you with stories of their own successes and failures. This is a great way to take some pressure off of yourself and your children.

Finally, remember to communicate with your children on subjects other than discipline. The better rapport you have with your children, the easier it will be to help them control their behavior. You will likely find that allocating just 15 minutes a day for you and your child to have a quiet talk will significantly improve your relationship and enhance your child's self-esteem.

There are many ways to communicate with your child. Try to have conversations about areas of common interest. Read to your child and discuss the stories. Play games. Let your child know about your job—what you do and how you feel about it. Share some anecdotes about the people you work with. Share your hobbies and interests with your children. They will feel honored by this sharing and show of confidence in them.

As we said earlier, children are very sensitive to your stress level. Improving your ability to cope with stress will help your child. As you read this book with your own children, you will undoubtedly find some ideas that will help you reduce your own stress. By practicing some relaxation techniques on a regular basis and identifying and actively coping with stressors in your own life, you will greatly aid your children in reducing their own stress.

Reducing stressful situations between yourself and your spouse is one major way in which you can help reduce your child's stress. You can do this by trying to improve your communication skills with your spouse. It is good for children to watch people positively working out their differences of opinion. If you feel there are some topics that are too volatile for a calm discussion, try to save the fireworks for a time when your children are not likely to be viewers and participants.

Children often feel that they are to blame for what happens between their parents. In general, you can help your child understand when something is his or her responsibility and when it is not. For example, if you are having problems with your spouse, it may be important to reassure your child that he or she is not the cause of these problems.

If you find that you are overreacting to your child's behavior, you may want to let your child know that you're aware of your behavior and discuss the events when you are calmer. Remember that if you can cope effectively with your own stress, you will be modeling positive and assertive behavior for your children as well as relieving them of the need to cope with your stress in addition to theirs. This is one of the best gifts you can give to your child.

EVEN STRESS HAS ITS GOOD POINTS!

Hans Selye, who first emphasized the importance of stress on the psyche, explained how stress affects us even when good things happen. Selye suggested that rather than trying to eradicate stress from our lives, we must learn how to use the stress in order to grow, as a challenge for developing new coping skills, and to increase our sense of mastery.

When you help your child learn to manage stress, you are giving him or her one of the keys to living a full and fulfilling life. We wish you much success in this endeavor!

WHEN TO SEEK PROFESSIONAL HELP FOR CHILDREN UNDER STRESS

It is our belief that many people can help children with psychological issues. Parents, teachers, grandparents, neighbors, and friends of the family have always been the primary influences on the emotional development of children, through good times and bad. The significant people in a child's life can enhance their natural helping abilities through self-help books and other parenting tools.

Some children, however, need more. Each child has a unique personality and a unique ability to cope with stress. Just as some children need extra help in math or spelling, others need extra help in coping with even "normal" amounts of stress.

There are many people trained to help children and their families with problems. These include psychologists, psychiatrists, social workers, family therapists, pastoral counselors, school psychologists, and others. Some of the most common sources of referrals are pediatricians, school principals, and school psychologists. When choosing professionals to help you and your children, make sure that they have experience in helping families deal with stress, and make sure that you are comfortable with them.

Sometimes a family in crisis selects a helping professional impulsively, in order to get relief as soon as possible. Although it is often difficult, we strongly recommend that you take time in making your decision and that you interview two or three professionals and choose the one whom you feel is most qualified.

It is *normal* for children to have some problems: to be afraid sometimes, to worry sometimes, even to sometimes have stress-induced aches and pains. But a child or family may need professional help if these problems are unusually intense, are prolonged in duration, cause significant physical symptoms, or interfere with the normal, day-to-day tasks of childhood.

Place a check mark by any of these statements that describe a child about whom you are concerned.

PROBLEM CHECKLIST

_____ The child shows a pronounced loss of appetite, change of sleeping habits, or other disturbance in his or her day-to-day routine.

_____ The child seems angry or depressed all the time.

_____ The child has new difficulties in school, either socially or academically.

_____ The child is argumentative or defiant.

_____ The child wishes to be alone most of the time.

_____ The child displays constant physical symptoms, including— but not limited to—stomach aches, tics, constant tiredness, aches and pains, and headaches.

_____ The child has sudden mood swings.

_____ The child has a very negative view about everything and often says negative things about himself or herself.

_____ The child shows an unusual degree of worry and anxiety.

_____ The child seems tense and worried much of the time.

_____ The child has difficulty relating to adults and/or other children.

If you check even *one* of these statements, you should consult a mental heath professional.

If there is any indication at all that your child may need extra help, we urge you to consult a professional. He or she will be the best person to help you evaluate your situation objectively and judge which problems will diminish with time and which need more attention. You can also check out *When Your Child Needs Help: A Parent's Guide to Therapy for Children*, a helpful resource by Dr. Norma Doft (Harmony Books, 1992).

ABOUT THE AUTHORS

Laura Slap-Shelton, Psy.D., is a licensed clinical psychologist with a specialty in neuropsychology. She graduated from Hahnemann University's graduate clinical psychology program in 1988. She consults, teaches, writes, and has a private practice in Lafayette Hill, Pennsylvania, where she lives with her daughter.

Lawrence E. Shapiro, Ph.D., has had more than 15 years working with children as a teacher, school psychologist, director of a school for special-needs children, and in private practice. He is the author of over two dozen books and therapeutic games. Dr. Shapiro is also the president of the Childswork/Childsplay catalog, the country's largest distributor of therapeutic games, toys, and books.

Hennie M. Shore has edited or written articles for various trade and consumer magazines and periodicals. Currently she is the senior editor of *The Child Therapy News*, which is published six times yearly by Childswork/Childsplay, and the author or co-author of many other psychologically oriented materials produced by Childswork/Childsplay. Ms. Shore lives in Wynnewood, Pennsylvania, with her husband and two children.

ABOUT THE ARTIST

Bob Beckett, a resident of Cherry Hill, New Jersey, has been a cartoonist/designer for over 30 years. He has done numerous illustrations for children's books, greeting cards, newspapers, and advertising and educational materials. He has been an award-winning television graphics designer at WCAU-TV in Philadelphia since 1960.